MINDFUL ME

MINDFULNESS AT SCHOOL

BY AMBER BULLIS, MLIS

BLUE OWL
BOOKS

TIPS FOR CAREGIVERS

Social and emotional learning (SEL) helps children manage emotions, learn how to feel empathy, create and achieve goals, and make good decisions. An important goal of teaching SEL skills is providing students with ways to be aware of and manage their emotions. Using mindfulness practices can help support these skills, both in and outside of the classroom or school setting.

BEFORE READING

Talk to the reader about tools he or she uses to calm down or focus in school.

Discuss: Do you ever have a hard time focusing at school? What are ways you can help your mind and body get ready for learning?

AFTER READING

Talk to the reader about mindfulness at school.

Discuss: What are some ways you can be mindful at school? How could these practices help you outside of school, too?

SEL GOAL

Children are more likely to struggle with self-regulation during times of transition, such as from one class to the next, from one activity to another, and from lunch back to learning. Try practicing mindfulness to help these transitions go more smoothly. Set aside a few moments at the beginning of class for students to shut their eyes and focus on breathing. Students will have the opportunity to reset and focus for the next lesson.

TABLE OF CONTENTS

CHAPTER 1

A TIME FOR MINDFULNESS

Recess is over. You race back to your classroom. It is time to sit down for the next lesson. But your body feels busy. It's hard to sit still. This is a good time to practice **mindfulness**!

Are you excited about something? Maybe tomorrow is a class field trip. You think about how fun it will be. It's hard to **focus** on school.

It is normal for your mind to wander. Recognize that you lost focus. Then bring your mind back to school. What are you working on? What is the next step? Mindfulness is being **aware** of the present moment. It helps you pay attention and focus.

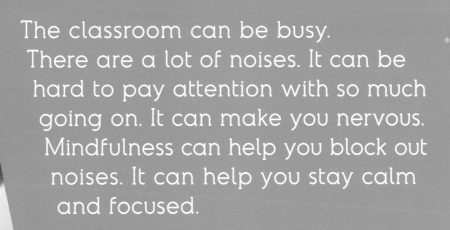

The classroom can be busy. There are a lot of noises. It can be hard to pay attention with so much going on. It can make you nervous. Mindfulness can help you block out noises. It can help you stay calm and focused.

3-3-3 RULE

If your mind feels too busy, try the 3-3-3 rule. Look around. Name 3 things you see. Then listen. Name 3 sounds. Then focus on 3 body parts. These tricks can help calm you down.

You can't find the answer to a math problem. You start to feel upset. This is another time to practice mindfulness. Close your eyes, and take deep breaths. **Inhale** through your nose. **Exhale**. Do this breathing exercise 5 times. Do you feel relaxed? Does your mind feel more clear? This is mindfulness.

ASK FOR HELP

Keep trying to find the answer yourself. But if you still can't, don't be afraid to ask for help. It is good to ask questions! This can help you learn.

CHAPTER 2

HOW IT HELPS

Mindfulness helps us **manage** our **emotions**. It helps us be more **intentional** with our words and actions. Maybe you are working on a team project. Others aren't listening to your ideas. You feel frustrated.

Take a second to breathe.
This calms you down.
You decide to listen.
You try their idea. It works!

Are you feeling left out at recess? This makes you mad. You want to yell. Instead, you pause. You take a few deep breaths. Is yelling the best way to **react**? After you calm down, you ask your friends if you can play. They say yes!

Being mindful can help us be **patient**. We take turns. We raise our hands before we answer. We respect those around us. We respect their ideas, too.

CHAPTER 3

PRACTICE IT!

You can practice mindfulness every day! Mindfulness is taking time to **reflect**. Pause to write down how you feel.

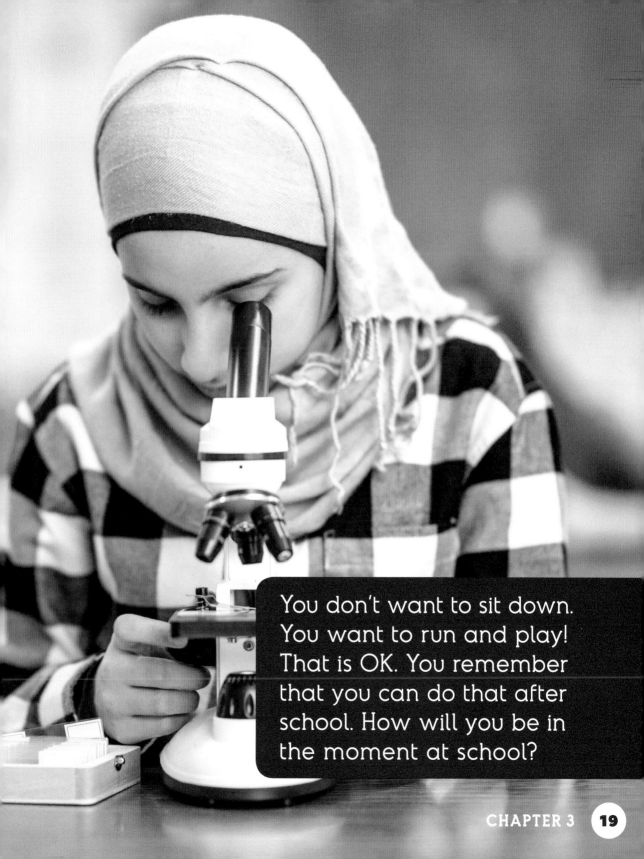

You don't want to sit down. You want to run and play! That is OK. You remember that you can do that after school. How will you be in the moment at school?

Does your class practice **meditation**? You can do it together! Close your eyes. Focus on your breathing. Inhale deeply through the nose. Exhale. You can all start to calm down. You are ready to learn!

TAKE THE LEAD!

Does your teacher lead meditation? Ask if you can lead it one day! You and your classmates can take turns. How will you help your peers be mindful?

GOALS AND TOOLS

GROW WITH GOALS

There are many ways to practice mindfulness at school.

Goal: Tell your teacher! Share with your teacher what you learned about mindfulness. Ask if you can practice it together as a classroom.

Goal: Practice gratitude! Write down one thing you are thankful for every day for one week. Try to focus on things you are grateful for at school. See how this makes you feel.

Goal: Try new ways to be mindful! If you like to meditate, try to journal. If you like to focus on how your body feels, try to pay attention to your mind. You might like something new!

MINDFULNESS EXERCISE

Using mindfulness at school can help you pay attention and learn more. Before each class, pause to take a few deep breaths. Reset yourself for the next subject.

1. Does your mind feel more clear?

2. How does your body feel at the beginning of class?

3. What are other ways you can practice mindfulness at school?

GLOSSARY

aware
Noticing and being conscious
of something.

emotions
Feelings, such as happiness,
anger, or sadness.

exhale
To breathe out.

focus
To concentrate on something.

inhale
To breathe in.

intentional
Purposeful or deliberate.

manage
To work upon or try to alter.

meditation
The act of thinking deeply
and quietly.

mindfulness
A mentality achieved by focusing
on the present moment and calmly
recognizing and accepting your
feelings, thoughts, and sensations.

patient
Able to put up with problems
or delays without getting angry
or upset.

react
To behave in a particular way
as a response to something that
has happened.

reflect
To think carefully or seriously
about something.

TO LEARN MORE

**FACT
SURFER**

Finding more information is as easy as 1, 2, 3.

1. Go to www.factsurfer.com

2. Enter "**mindfulnessatschool**" into the search box.

3. Choose your cover to see a list of websites.

INDEX

Blue Owl Books are published by Jump!, 5357 Penn Avenue South, Minneapolis, MN 55419, www.jumplibrary.com

Copyright © 2020 Jump! International copyright reserved in all countries. No part of this book may be reproduced in any form without written permission from the publisher.

Library of Congress Cataloging-in-Publication Data

Names: Bullis, Amber, author.
Title: Mindfulness at school / Amber Bullis.
Description: Minneapolis, MN: Jump!, Inc., [2020] | Series: Mindful me
Includes index. | Audience: Ages 7–10
Identifiers: LCCN 2019022738 (print)
LCCN 2019022739 (ebook)
ISBN 9781645271727 (hardcover)
ISBN 9781645271734 (paperback)
ISBN 9781645271741 (ebook)
Subjects: LCSH: Mindfulness (Psychology) | Emotions in children. | School children—Psychology.
Classification: LCC BF637.M56 B85 2020 (print)
LCC BF637.M56 (ebook) | DDC 155.4/124—dc23
LC record available at https://lccn.loc.gov/2019022738
LC ebook record available at https://lccn.loc.gov/2019022739

Editor: Jenna Trnka
Designer: Molly Ballanger

Photo Credits: iofoto/Shutterstock, cover (girl); Africa Studio/Shutterstock, cover (backpack), 4, 5, 6–7; Samuel Borges Photography/Shutterstock, 1; Simplylove/Shutterstock, 3; JackF/iStock, 8–9; ESB Professional/Shutterstock, 10–11; SDI Productions/iStock, 12, 13; Aaron-H/iStock, 14; FatCamera/iStock, 14–15, 19; lisegagne/iStock, 16–17; KK Tan/Shutterstock, 18; Wavebreakmedia/iStock, 20–21.

Printed in the United States of America at Corporate Graphics in North Mankato, Minnesota.